DRUGS
THE COMPLETE STORY

COCAINE

Sarita Kendall

STECK-VAUGHN
L I B R A R Y
A Division of Steck-Vaughn Company

Austin, Texas

CONTENTS

"Cocaine's the worst drug problem we've ever had in the U.S. . . . it's devastating."

Some miners chew twice as much coca as a regular user.

"It was the only crop that earned us enough money to buy food, clothes, and medicines."

"Every time we went to attack the labs, our helicopters were hit by machine-gun fire."

CONTENTS

GLOSSARY

addict: a person who relies on a drug and needs to use more and more of it to stay "high." If an addict stops taking the drug, he or she may have physical withdrawal symptoms, such as vomiting, and psychological symptoms, such as depression.

alkaloid: one of a group of substances found in the leaves of plants that contain the chemicals nitrogen, oxygen, carbon, and hydrogen. Cocaine, caffeine, and nicotine are all alkaloids.

coca: the leaf that contains cocaine, used in making cocaine hydrochloride and crack.

cocaine: the alkaloid or drug content of the coca leaf. Often "cocaine" is used to refer to "cocaine hydrochloride."

cocaine hydrochloride: refined cocaine from the coca leaf, this is sometimes a fine white powder or a rocklike slab. Also known as "coke," *perica* (Colombia), "snow", and "toot." It is usually sniffed, or a solution of cocaine powder is injected.

cocaine paste: a crude, grayish paste produced after the first stage of processing coca leaves.

crack: the highly-addictive smokable form of cocaine, made by mixing cocaine hydrochloride with bicarbonate of soda. Usually in white or brownish chunks, it is also called "rock."

cut: to lessen the strength of cocaine by mixing it with another white powder, such as talcum powder. Street dealers often cut cocaine to increase the amount of the drug that they can sell.

freebase: when cocaine paste is refined, the result is cocaine base. "Base" is usually referred to as "paste" in South America, particularly among the people who smoke it. Other local words are *basuco* (Colombia) and *pitillo* (Peru, Bolivia).

mule: the name used to describe drug couriers.

pusher: someone who sells drugs illegally.

speedball: a mixture of cocaine and heroin or morphine.

1

COCA AND COCAINE

Cocaine is made from the leaves of the coca plant. The drug produces an emotional lift, then a "down." At first, users experience a "high" or "rush" that makes them feel smart, lively, and excited. However, the buzz is soon followed by a depression or "crash" and the feeling that only more cocaine will cure it. Thus a habit can begin that is very hard to escape.

The deadly trap

The people who produce and sell cocaine are caught in a trap. The smugglers and dealers earn so much money from the drug that no legal business can compete. The peasants who grow the coca leaves often plant coca rather than food crops, because coca brings in a better income. However, with no one growing corn, beans, and bananas, it becomes more and more expensive to feed the family. In the end, the peasant families are often poorer than they would have been if they had grown food crops.

> *The people who produce and sell the drug are in a trap.*

South America now produces so much cocaine that the drug has become alarmingly cheap and easy to buy. Although cocaine is illegal, at least one out of every ten Americans has tried it. The Colombian city of Medellín is the center of the international cocaine trade. Tons of cocaine are channeled through Medellín to the United States and Europe every year supplying the demand.

COCAINE

The coca plant was from Peru but is now grown widely in South America. Cocaine is extracted from the leaves.

Bolivia, Colombia, and Peru produce most of the world's cocaine. From the deep, tropical valleys of the Andes mountains to the streets of New York, London, and Sydney, hundreds of thousands of people are directly involved in the cocaine trade. This chain of involvement includes the peasant coca farmers, the cocaine "cooks," the dealers, the gunmen, the pilots, the money men, and the traffickers. Colombia's cocaine bosses run the biggest and most efficient trafficking networks in the world. With their money, they can control parts of the government, the economy, the military, and the judicial system. They also run whole regions of the country. Cocaine is not only grown, processed, and exported by Colombia, it is also snorted and smoked at every level of society. More than any other nation, Colombia shows the power of cocaine.

More than any other nation, Colombia shows the power of cocaine.

Cocaine damages health and kills

According to drug experts, over a million Americans are addicted to cocaine. They keep using the drug even though they know it is ruining their lives. Some users snort or inject the drug, but many smoke crack, a form of cocaine that has an even stronger, more immediate effect. Most crack users are between the ages of 18 and 35. Some are 10-year-old children unafraid of smoking something they associate with a cigarette.

"Snorting" cocaine powder into the nostril is a frequent method of taking the drug.

COCAINE

Not everyone who tries cocaine becomes a regular user or an addict. However, the great danger for cocaine and crack users is addiction, which can control all aspects of an addict's life. Mental and physical health are at stake. Cocaine and crack can cause medical problems or even death. A single dose of cocaine can sometimes result in seizures or heart failure.

> *"Cocaine's the worst drug problem we've ever had in the U.S. Among the young, it's devastating."*

"Cocaine's the worst drug problem we've ever had in the United States. Among the young, it's devastating. That's where you see the crime, the overdoses, and the deaths," says Dr. William McAuliffe of the Harvard Cocaine Project. "By the time you find out it's not harmless, it's too late."

THE COCA LEAF

Long before anyone discovered how to make cocaine, coca leaves had a special importance for people living in the mountains and forests of South America. According to one legend, the first three farmers of the region needed to clear some land for growing crops, so they set fire to the hillsides. The smoke rose, enveloping the mountain gods on the snow peaks and making them angry. The gods sent terrible rainstorms that washed away houses, fields, and footpaths. Families wandered everywhere searching for food until, exhausted and starving, they collapsed by some bushes and started eating the leaves. At once, they forgot they were hungry and felt strong enough to plant crops and rebuild their homes.

Chewing coca has been practiced for thousands of years. These antique pots show coca chewers with bulging cheeks.

COCAINE

Chewing coca leaves

Coca leaves are still chewed by more than three million men and women in Bolivia, Colombia, Peru, and the Amazon lowlands. Both the Bolivian and the Peruvian governments accept that there is a big difference between chewing coca and making cocaine. While the making and selling of cocaine is a criminal offense, coca chewing is still allowed in most areas. Coca chewing begins with the selection of a few dried leaves that are placed in the person's mouth, one by one. When they are moist with saliva, a little powdered lime is added to them. This frees the substances called alkaloids that are found in the leaves. Like most alkaloids, cocaine is made up of carbon, hydrogen, nitrogen, and oxygen, and has a strong effect on the body. Other alkaloids include caffeine (from coffee beans), nicotine (from tobacco leaves), and morphine (from opium poppies).

The rich green juice gradually released by the leaves has a stimulating effect.

A wad of coca is often kept in the mouth for two hours or more. It is moved gently from one cheek to the other, rather than chewed up. The rich green juice gradually released by the leaves has a stimulating effect. It reduces tiredness and hunger and, for a time, makes the person feel good.

In addition to cocaine and other alkaloids, coca leaves also contain traces of calcium, iron, vitamins, and protein. These nutrients supplement the poor diet in the Andes mountains and allow the body to cope with high altitudes. Coca seems to help the lungs transfer the smaller amount of oxygen found in the thin mountain air to the red corpuscles in the blood. The oxygen carried by these red corpuscles is then distributed around the body. The amount of cocaine absorbed by a regular chewer of coca leaves is small.

Archaeologists have found evidence that coca was cultivated at least 4,000 years ago in western South America. Crumbling leaves and lime containers made of pottery and gold have been found in early graves. There are also old pottery figures of people chewing coca, with a bulge in one cheek.

When the Spaniards reached South America in 1538, they

reported that people had their mouths so filled with a green herb that they could hardly speak. At first the Spanish church leaders wanted to stop the use of coca because of its religious importance. They thought people would become Christians quicker if old customs were forbidden. However, they soon realized that, with coca, laborers worked harder and seemed to need less food. So the Spaniards themselves began to grow coca and make money by selling it to the miners and animal herders of the high Andes. As a result, coca chewing spread even more.

Coca, religion, and society

In both the Andes mountains and the valleys of the Amazon, coca has long been used at religious ceremonies. The Incas, who ruled over much of the Andes region until the Spaniards arrived in America, offered coca to their gods. Some farmers still sprinkle a few leaves on the land when asking for a good harvest.

Along the Brazilian Amazon frontier, the local forest tribes pound coca with ash, chanting stories about the coca plant while they work. Then the men smoke tobacco and chew the powdered coca mixture during the evening. They also use coca in special ceremonies, claiming that it helps them to stay in touch with their ancestors.

Among the Kogi tribe living in the Sierra Nevada mountains near the Caribbean coast, a young man is given his first lime container when he is considered to be an adult. Lime made from seashells is put in the container, which is shaped out of a gourd. The Kogi men chew coca during all-night sessions when they dance, recite myths, and discuss the community's problems. Chewing together makes people feel friendly and talkative.

Chewing together makes people feel friendly and talkative.

Carlos Huayta, who has a small shop in the Bolivian town of Coroico, believes like many others that coca is slightly magical. "When the leaves fall this way — freely, with the right side up — it's a good sign. If something's lost it will be found, or if my sister's traveling, I know she's all right."

COCAINE

Carlos also puts coca leaves in his shoes to help his arthritis. People in the lower Andean valleys often grow a few bushes near the house so they can make coca tea to treat headaches and stomachaches. The leaves also have a numbing effect and are packed on the gums to relieve toothaches.

Coca and work

Most of the people who use coca are farmers or miners, with heavy work to do. Sometimes laborers receive coca as part of their wages. The sugarcane harvesters of eastern Bolivia once called a strike because they had no leaves to chew.

To refuse to share coca leaves is extremely discourteous in traditional villages. Highland Peruvians often carry a *chuspa,* which is a small bag filled with coca leaves. Some chuspas have a coca leaf design woven into them. During a hard morning's digging for potatoes, a coca break is common. Each person gives a small bundle of leaves to the others. They blow on their leaves before they start chewing, making a wish for health or good luck.

The men working in Bolivia's tin and silver mines chew nearly twice as much coca as a normal user. They also offer leaves to the spirit guarding the mine, so that they will find rich

The Andean tin and silver miners chew the most coca. They say it stops tiredness and keeps their lungs clear.

veins of metal. In the Potosí mines, 12,000 feet above sea level, it is rare to meet anyone without a plastic bag of coca leaves stuffed into his pocket. "We can't work without it," says one miner on his way down the shaft. "Coca gives energy and health. If you're chewing, the dust and gas can't get into your lungs and make you sick."

> *Some miners chew twice as much coca as a regular user.*

However, not everyone agrees with this point of view. According to a mine owner in Potosí, those who chew four or five pounds of leaves a week become dull and zombielike. They do less work, not more, and they are slow to understand instructions. Until more studies are done, it is difficult to be certain of the effects of coca chewing on the mind and body.

> *It is difficult to be certain of the effects of coca chewing on the mind and body.*

Coca leaves are sold in many Andean towns and villages and chewed by a majority of the native population.

COCAINE

Coca and cocaine

Most people who chew coca, or use the leaves in other ways, have never tried cocaine. However, the fact that cocaine is illegal affects them in a number of ways. At times, it is difficult to obtain coca leaves because they have been bought up by cocaine manufacturers. People taking coca leaves from the growing areas to their homes may be stopped by the police and even jailed. In Peru, selling coca in areas that are below a height of 5,000 feet has been prohibited. As a result, chewing itself has virtually stopped.

A United Nations (U.N.) agreement to stamp out coca growing and chewing by 1989 was signed by several countries. The idea was that if coca could not be grown and used legally, then it would be easier to prevent cocaine production. However, banning the traditional use of coca in South America is like trying to stop coffee or tea drinking in North America and Europe. The tribes of the Amazon regions and the communities of the Andes fiercely defend their right to use coca.

GROWING COCA

Farmers can make more money from coca than almost any other crop in South America. Until the early 1970s, coca plantations were limited to a few areas. Neat terraces of bushes and lime-green patches dotted the eastern valleys of Bolivia and Peru. There were coca plants in gardens that were cultivated by Amazon Indians, and plants were grown in some parts of highland Colombia.

Small farmers pulled up sugarcane, coffee bushes, and even orange trees to grow coca.

Then, as cocaine suddenly became fashionable in the United States, the price of coca leaves jumped. New plantations sprouted along the Andes and in the lowlands as forests were cleared away. Small farmers pulled up sugarcane, coffee bushes, and even orange trees to grow coca. There is no other crop that needs so little attention. Coffee needs to be fertilized and tended carefully, and oranges do not keep well after they are picked.

Farming coca

There are several different varieties of coca. Some grow well on drier, stony hillsides up to a height of 5,000 feet, while others are suited to the hot, wet Amazon valley areas. The plants may be kept small (less than three feet tall) or left to grow big and bushy. Coca leaves are oval and light green in color. The plants have delicate white flowers and bright red seeds.

COCAINE

The steep mountainsides of the Yungas region of Bolivia are covered with stone terraces for coca cultivation. After some years coca makes the ground barren and the land erodes away.

Between 1972 and 1988, the area planted with coca increased more than 15 times. Bolivia and Peru, the main growing countries, probably have over 120,000 coca farmers. Brazil and Colombia, which used to grow very little, have also become important coca producers.

Farmers in areas where coca has traditionally been grown usually have small plots. The more recent settlers, moving from the Andes highlands down to the jungle, have cut down trees to plant huge areas with coca. A professor of agriculture at Lima University estimates that, taking into account all the land occupied by coca farmers and by people connected with the cocaine business, cocaine has meant the destruction of 1,700,000 acres of Amazon forest in Peru alone.

Cocaine traffickers often help to organize the farmers, giving them advice on how to produce bigger crops. Once coca is well established, there is guaranteed work harvesting the leaves. New communities, depending almost entirely on growing coca and selling it to the traffickers, have grown up in the vast jungle valleys and lowlands.

Substitute crops

When the coca leaves have been picked, they are usually spread out to dry, or they may be made into a rough cocaine paste immediately. At first, some coca growers did not realize what the leaves were being used for.

> *"It was the only crop that earned us enough money to buy food, clothes, and medicines."*

"I was living away from home. My mother came and told me everyone was planting something called coca, and it was good money . . . so of course we all got into it. It was the only crop that earned us enough money to buy food, clothes, and medicines," said Ramiro Robles, a farmer from the Cauca region of Colombia. Later on, he pulled up his bushes, when the U.N. started to run a special program in the area. By introducing new crops with good prices, the program encourages people to grow crops other than coca. Ramiro, who has only $7\frac{1}{2}$ acres of land, now grows corn, beans, and fruit. With U.N. help he has built a small fish-breeding pond.

It is not that farmers always make an enormous profit from coca, but rather that what they earn from other crops may be so little. Coca can be sold on the spot, whereas food products must be taken to distant markets. The areas where coca is grown are often far away from the main cities, with terrible roads and no regular transportation. People have to do without schools, medical centers, electricity, and drinking water.

To get rid of coca, substituting new crops and building the roads, dams, and hospitals needed to improve the quality of people's lives is too expensive for South American governments to undertake on their own. Nations like the U.S., the U.K., and some European countries are supporting the U.N. and other programs to reduce cocaine production.

Grants have been given to coca farmers to encourage them to grow coffee (as shown here) and other crops.

The antidrug police patrols try to destroy illegal coca plantations wherever they find them. However, it takes a long time to burn the crop and the plants often grow again.

However, it is slow work, and cocaine traffickers have both the money and the weapons to attack anticoca projects. The Huallaga valley of eastern Peru had over 170,000 acres planted with coca. Peruvian antidrug patrols cut down the bushes one by one and burned them. The farmers were given bank loans to grow cocoa and other food crops. Yet, over five years, only 30,000 acres of coca were destroyed, and new plantations appeared in the more distant parts of the valley. More than 20 people connected with the project were murdered by drug gangs during this time.

"It takes 60 men a whole day to get rid of 2 $\frac{1}{2}$ acres of coca."

Brazilian and Colombian police also destroy coca plantations when they discover them hidden away in the jungle. However, the patrols have to be flown in by helicopter, or spend days traveling there by canoe. It takes 60 men a whole day to get rid of 2 $\frac{1}{2}$ acres of coca. Even then, this method is not very effective: "The police came and cut down the bushes and burned them, but the roots are strong, and the coca grew back right away, giving better harvests than ever," said one Colombian farmer.

Bolivian coca growers

Coca was grown in the Bolivian valleys, or Yungas, at least 600 years ago. In some places, the old stone terraces built by the Incas on the mountainsides can still be seen. Coca is legally grown here, and the dried leaves are packed into large bales to be sent to Potosí and other highland cities. However, some farmers sell their leaves to cocaine traffickers when they are offered attractive prices.

In the Yungas, 2 $\frac{1}{2}$ acres of coca will yield about 350 kilograms (770 pounds) of leaves during the year. The bushes go on producing for more than 15 years, but they take all the fertility out of the soil, making it difficult to grow anything else afterward. "Bare hillsides appear. No other crop in the world causes similar levels of erosion," said one researcher at Peru's national agrarian university in Lima.

Farther south, in the Chapare region, yields are much higher — over 2,200 pounds of leaves can be harvested from each

COCAINE

2¹/₂ acres. Nearly all the coca in this area is used for making cocaine. Although coca prices bounce up and down according to how much the traffickers are paying, coca is nearly always more profitable than other crops.

"No other crop in the world causes similar levels of erosion."

In the early 1980s, the Chapare peasants enjoyed a real coca boom. Thousands of people from the poor highlands went to live in the area, hoping to make their fortunes. Most of the money they earned was spent on televisions, motor bikes, stereo systems, and other luxury goods. So little food was being grown that it had to be brought in from other places and prices suddenly skyrocketed. By this time too much coca was being produced, and farmers had difficulty selling it. They were left with electric ovens and televisions for which there was no electricity. Many people were worse off than they had been before the boom.

Bolivia's peasants are determined to go on growing coca. Coca growers have held huge marches, blocked the roads, and taken over government offices in protest against the plans to limit coca farming. A law passed by the Bolivian congress says that nearly all the Chapare plantations must be replaced by other crops, but farmers in the Yungas who produce leaves for traditional use can keep their coca. One of the main problems in making this law work is that Bolivia is too poor a country to pay for projects that would allow the Chapare farmers to earn a living in other ways. So far, the money from the U.N. is not nearly enough.

4

PROCESSING COCAINE

Until the nineteenth century, nobody understood exactly what substance in the coca leaf made coca chewing so popular in South America. However, between 1855 and 1860, two German scientists, Friedrich Gaedecke and Albert Niemann, independently of one another, extracted an alkaloid from coca leaves. They called this alkaloid cocaine.

Once cocaine could be manufactured, it was sold in many different forms. Mariani's wine (patented in 1863), was strengthened with cocaine and was drunk by famous people. Nose sprays, chewing gum, lozenges, soft drinks, tonics, and quack medicines sold without any prescription contained cocaine. At the beginning of this century, the U.S. was importing about 10 tons of cocaine a year.

In 1914, the U.S. passed a law that labeled cocaine a dangerous drug.

Although many doctors saw cocaine as a new wonder drug, others warned that it could lead to poisoning and addiction. Opinions swung against cocaine, and the soft drink Coca-Cola was changed to leave in coca leaf flavoring without including the alkaloid itself. In 1914, the U.S. passed a law that labeled cocaine a dangerous drug and introduced strict controls. Two years later, the U.K. also outlawed cocaine. A little of the drug is still manufactured legally for medical purposes, particularly as an anesthetic for eye operations.

The rest of the world's cocaine (more than 99 percent) comes from illegal laboratories. Most of these are hidden

21

COCAINE

away in western South America. The lab may consist of three plastic buckets, some sacking, and the chemicals needed to make a few grams (ounces) of crude paste, or it may be a well-organized camp with the best equipment, turning out 50 kilograms (110 pounds) of refined white powder a week.

... three plastic buckets, some sacking, and the chemicals ... make a few grams of crude paste ...

The cocaine kitchen

Coca leaves are bulky to transport, so the first stage of processing them into cocaine paste is normally done close to the plantation. "There are as many different ways of processing cocaine as there are laboratories," said one experienced cocaine cook. The labs are often known as kitchens, and cocaine cooks have their favorite recipes.

Generally, it takes between 150 and 250 kilograms (330 and 550 pounds) of leaves to make two pounds of paste. The leaves are mixed with a strong alkali such as caustic soda and well trampled for an hour or so to release the alkaloids. Then the mixture is added to kerosene or gasoline. When hundreds of pounds are being processed, plastic sheeting is staked out on the ground to make a huge bathtub. Otherwise, an ordinary oil drum can be used.

"There are as many different ways of processing cocaine as there are laboratories."

Within a few hours, the alkaloids have dissolved into the gasoline. The leaves are strained off and squeezed to get all the liquid from them. An acid (usually diluted sulfuric acid) has to be churned into the gasoline mixture so the alkaloids will separate out. When they have passed from the gasoline into the water, the mixture is filtered to produce a brown, sludgy paste.

The paste contains between 20 and 50 percent pure cocaine, according to the variety of leaves and the chemicals used. The next stage, converting crude paste into the high-grade paste

Since the simplest equipment is needed to turn coca leaves into paste, cocaine "kitchens" can be set up anywhere.

called freebase, needs greater knowledge and can easily go wrong. Some farmers know how to make the freebase. However, the coca farmers are often visited by a dealer who buys the paste and passes a whole batch on to a more sophisticated lab where the impurities are taken out.

For the final stage, when the base is refined into cocaine hydrochloride crystals, special chemicals such as ether and acetone are needed. A large refining lab typically has a lot of equipment, including glass beakers, accurate weighing scales, coffee filter papers, instruments for measuring the purity of the chemicals, rubber hoses, and microwave ovens for drying cocaine powder. The lab may be hidden away in a city apartment building, camouflaged by trees in the Amazon forest, or moved from one place to another to try to fool the authorities. Police have discovered labs in nearly all the South and Central American countries, but there are probably more in Colombia than anywhere else.

COCAINE

El Raudal, Colombia, became a center for importing chemicals to produce cocaine in the jungle laboratories.

The biggest Colombian cocaine-making complexes have been disbanded in the eastern plains or Llanos. In September 1988, antidrug police launched Operation Canaguaro after receiving information about suspicious planes flying in and out of an isolated area. Three secret airstrips and five cocaine labs that processed leaves into cocaine hydrochloride were discovered and destroyed.

Apart from all the lab equipment and arms, the police also found a large number of documents, some containing the names of people connected with Colombia's biggest cocaine trafficking group, based in the city of Medellín. Tons of cocaine had been flown out by small planes to Central American countries, especially Guatemala, and from there to the U.S. Strangely, no one was captured during Operation Canaguaro. The people working in the labs must have had warning of the operation, or the noise of helicopters approaching was enough to send everyone racing into the jungle.

Most of those who work in the big labs never see their real bosses. The powerful traffickers have very little to do with the actual manufacture of cocaine. The lab workers are often unemployed young men from the poorest areas of Medellín and other Colombian cities. At the camps, there is TV, the food is free, and ordinary workers earn about twice as much as they would elsewhere. Sometimes part of the workers' wages is given in cocaine paste, which can be sold off at a profit.

San José del Guaviare

For ten years until 1988, San José del Guaviare in Colombia was the center of one of South America's biggest cocaine-producing regions. Planes jostled for space at the town's airport and large canoes lined the riverbanks. People from highland Colombia moved in, hoping to hit the jackpot, and some of them did.

San José became a very dangerous town, with murders on the streets and shootouts in broad daylight. The small police force could do little to control the violence. Chemicals for processing coca into cocaine were flown in openly and sent out to jungle labs. One police lieutenant reported, "Every time we went to attack the labs, our helicopters were hit by machine-gun fire."

> *"Every time we went to attack the labs, our helicopters were hit by machine-gun fire."*

Armed Communist rebels began to take over the region. They charged a tax on each kilogram* of cocaine, and in return they guarded the coca fields and labs. Some were involved in organizing cocaine exports to other countries. Up river from San José, at El Raudal, the rebels were in complete control. However, as the Colombian army moved into San José and began to search boats and planes, it became more difficult to ship in chemicals for the labs.

Cocaine cooks began to experiment with substances that could be bought without arousing suspicion. They used cement instead of lime, because it was easy to say that the cement was for building. They found that fertilizers, which contain nitrogen, served as the alkali for turning paste into freebase. They had to use low-grade gasoline that contained high levels of lead. The lead from low-grade gas is particularly dangerous and can cause damage to a person's lungs, brain, and muscles. All this experimentation meant that it took nearly a week to process a batch of cocaine around El Raudal.

*Metric measure is usually used for drugs.

COCAINE

Then, in 1988, the army forced the rebels out of the area and destroyed many of the plantations and labs. Many families suddenly became unemployed. Some moved farther into the jungle and started all over again, out of reach of the army. "We've already got more coca planted 60 miles away," said one cocaine maker from El Raudal. Some cut their coca patches out of the forest in a national park, which was supposed to be a nature reserve. Although the boom in San José was over, many people felt that their lives had improved. They could walk through the town without meeting gunmen, and the government was talking about encouraging different crops and building new roads.

Sophisticated laboratories are often set up in the jungle to convert crude paste into high-grade freebase. This inferno is all that remains of a laboratory discovered and destroyed in Chapare, Bolivia.

THE PASTE PLAGUE

Wherever cocaine is made, it becomes available. People both young and old in the countries that produce cocaine can buy the paste very cheaply. Bolivia, Colombia, and Peru have recognized that they are developing serious drug use problems, and other nations are also affected. For example, in Brazil, where marijuana has been widely smoked for a long time, cocaine use is growing fast.

The paste smoked by South Americans is a whitish gray or light brown powder. The paste is actually the cocaine base that is produced after the second stage of the processing of coca leaves, rather than the crude sludge from the first stage. Although paste and crack are very alike in their immediate effects, paste still contains many chemical impurities that are taken out in the last stage of processing.

Paste is normally mixed with tobacco and smoked in a cigarette. The smoker enjoys a sudden high, but that feeling of energetic excitement lasts only for about five minutes. Then the downer begins to take hold, with unpleasant, anxious feelings. Because the downer is so uncomfortable and depressing, smokers want to get high again right away. This leads them to smoke more and more paste.

Sometimes people try to avoid the downers by mixing paste with marijuana, the dried leaves of the Cannabis plant. On top of this they may drink beer or liquor. Younger people may sniff glue, which is cheaper and easier to obtain, to try and smooth the ups and downs of paste smoking. Heavier smokers are very likely to be multidrug users.

A dealer in Bogotá, Colombia, described how a surgeon became so addicted to paste that he had to sell everything, including his car and his house, to pay for his habit. He even abandoned his family. When he tried to sell his watch, the only thing of value left, even the dealer was horrified and would not let him have any more paste.

Some Peruvian doctors carried out a study of paste-smoking addicts with serious health problems. Most of the patients were young men between 16 and 25 years old. More than half of them were students or unemployed. They were very thin and pale and had practically no interest in life apart from getting more paste to smoke. They did not want to share their cigarettes, so they usually smoked on their own.

The downer begins to take hold, with unpleasant, anxious feelings.

The patients explained how they alternated between excitement and anxiety when they were on paste. They also said that they became talkative and had difficulty sleeping. If they went on smoking they often saw and heard things that were not really there. These hallucinations sometimes made them think they were being followed by shadows that were trying to kill them. Other patients found themselves scratching at imaginary insects crawling on their skin. Three of the patients died — two were poisoned by paste and had badly damaged lungs, the third killed himself.

The spread of paste smoking is quite recent and astonishingly rapid. Paste use is now more common in the Andean countries than cocaine sniffing. Cocaine itself is more likely to be sniffed or "snorted" on special occasions. Although cocaine sniffing leads more gradually to dependence and does not contain the poisons in paste, it can be just as destructive.

The fight against cocaine

The cocaine-producing countries have begun to organize anti-drug marches, concerts, and national campaigns. Few surveys have been done, so it is difficult to know how many people are using cocaine. Also, the situation changes fast. An Ecuadorean street dealer in Quito started by selling marijuana but found that his customers were asking for paste. Within a few months he was selling nothing but paste.

According to the Bogotá city health department, over 50,000

people in the city have serious cocaine or cocaine paste addiction problems. About half a million of the Colombian capital's inhabitants — that is, one in ten — are at risk, because they have tried drugs or live among people who use them regularly.

Many antidrug programs are aimed at young people. In the Yungas of Bolivia, an Italian group has worked with teenage boys, who are encouraged to take an interest in carpentry, sports, and other activities. The young men started a local soccer championship and all the villagers turned out to watch.

Paste smoking was a serious problem in the Cauca region of Colombia. As the coca growers changed over to other crops with the backing of the U.N. program, there was less paste available. Community schools put on plays to show how cocaine had harmed their families. The plays had dramatic deaths and even suicides in them, because smoking and dealing in paste had led to a lot of violence in the area. For a local music competition, people composed songs telling how they had stopped growing coca and using paste.

A successful antidrug day was organized in Bogotá to educate people about the dangers of cocaine. The day was aimed at young people, since one in ten are at risk there.

COCAINE

The most successful programs seem to be those in which everybody decides together what to do about drugs. In some schools in Bogotá, teachers and students collect information and opinions about drugs, or organize a dance and music group, or perhaps a volleyball team. A program like this is not just a question of a talk once a year. It gives people information that is specific and truthful and helps them to find out for themselves what the problems are in their own immediate neighborhood.

> *"I hope you won't even think of me, Señora Drug . . . we finished our friendship, and I'm happy to have left you."*

One Colombian teenager wrote a letter to "Señora Drug." "I'm writing you this letter to tell you I don't want to know you. I don't want your friendship. You've already taken some of my friends almost to death." Another boy from the same class wrote: "I'm studying and learning to be a mechanic. I hope you won't even think of me, Señora Drug. A year and a half ago we finished our friendship, and I'm happy to have left you."

One problem in the prevention of drug use is that education experts are often frustrated about what to do. For example, a poster of 12 pictures showing how a person changes into a sick scarecrow with drug abuse was pasted up in the streets of Bogotá. To those who were not heavy users, it seemed ridiculous; they said they could never end up like that. Those already in a bad way from smoking paste joked about it and compared notes on how far they had traveled along the road to becoming a scarecrow themselves.

There are a few rehabilitation centers for heavy paste smokers who know they need help. However, most are expensive, and even after treatment many users return to paste smoking. David, a young musician, has been in treatment four times. He only has to smell paste while walking down the street to lose all his willpower and start smoking again.

Children on the streets of Bogotá

Some of the Bogotá street children who smoke paste have not even reached their teens. Ricardo, who is nine years old and wasting away, smokes between six and ten grams of paste (making 25 to 40 cigarettes) a day when he can get it. He begs in the city center, saying he needs money because he's hungry. He looks so young and pathetic that people sometimes offer to buy him food, but he always tries to persuade them to give him money instead. He uses the money to buy paste.

> *He begs in the city center, saying he needs money because he's hungry.*

Marta, who is 11 years old, also lives on the street and smokes about five grams of paste a day. Like other street children, Marta and Ricardo steal when they cannot get enough money from begging. They often run errands for drug dealers in exchange for paste. They trick the dealer's clients, too. Cars draw up near the dealing point and the client hands over some money to one of the children to go get the paste. It is easy for the child to scoop some powder out of the packet into a pocket then deliver the packet and ask for a tip.

Nine-year-old Ricardo and 11-year-old Marta are already heavy paste smokers. They live on the streets and, like other paste smokers, they are pathetically thin.

COCAINE

There are frequent police raids on paste houses, but the dealers are often back on the streets within a few days.

Thieves, prostitutes, and users meet at the dealer's house to smoke paste and marijuana. Marta takes her little supply of paste around the corner and hides in a shack to make her cigarettes. She wants to keep the paste for herself, but often another child will find her and force her to share it.

The police raid the paste houses regularly, hauling truckloads of dealers and users off to jail. Usually the dealers are back on the street within a few days, setting up their business nearby. When the children are taken into custody, the police cut their hair and hose them down before letting them go.

Marta and Ricardo sleep under bridges and in doorways and live on food scraps from restaurants and garbage cans. If they stop smoking for a while, they gain weight. However, there is little help for the young paste smokers. Most programs for street children are voluntary, and the paste addicts do not want to go into institutions. They know that their drug use may kill them, but they cannot stop it.

NATIONS IN DANGER

It is impossible to calculate exactly how much money the cocaine traffickers make, how they spend it, and where they keep it. The drug lords who organize the dealing and the smuggling operations keep much of their money outside South America. The money is "laundered," or cleaned up, by passing it into foreign banks, properties in the U.S. and the Caribbean, and many other businesses.

However, financial experts believe that between one billion and two billion U.S. dollars goes back into the Andean countries as a result of drug exports. Cocaine earns more for Bolivia and Peru than any other product of these countries that is legally exported.

> The traffickers' enormous fortunes are their most powerful weapon. They can buy almost anything they want.

The traffickers' enormous fortunes are their most powerful weapon. They can buy almost anything they want, and this is the great threat to the nations in the cocaine network. The influence of the drug traffickers in all countries, in the economy and in politics, is growing all the time.

South American nations owe so much money that many welcome any extra earnings, regardless of their source. People are allowed to change foreign money without explaining where it has come from. The governments have also made many tax allowances that make it possible for traffickers to bring back their illegal earnings.

COCAINE

How cocaine money is used

Cocaine profits are invested in many ways. Some are very obvious and showy, others more secretive and damaging. Well-known traffickers, including those wanted in the U.S. for cocaine smuggling, own huge luxurious properties in the cities and private zoos and ranches in the countryside. They have bought hotels, restaurants, pharmacies, and car rental businesses. They smuggle expensive cars, horses, and electronic equipment into the countries where they live.

Cocaine money has also been invested in banks, industries, newspapers, and television stations. By controlling the shares in a large industry or a television company the traffickers can have a strong influence over what is produced or what is said. The editor of one of Colombia's best-known newspapers, *El Espectador,* was murdered for his campaign against drugs, and the newspaper's offices and printing presses were bombed.

> *They smuggle expensive cars, horses, and electronic equipment into the country.*

Perhaps the most dangerous effect of cocaine money is the way it leads to widespread dishonesty and corruption. In countries where many people earn small salaries, traffickers can bribe prison officers to free them, customs agents to look the other way, police officers to protect their laboratories, and judges to declare them innocent.

Traffickers can also buy their way into politics, either by financing election campaigns for politicians who then owe them favors, or by running for office themselves. In their hometowns, traffickers often win support by helping people to find jobs, and they donate money for local activities like house-building or sponsoring a soccer team.

Senior government officials are often involved in the cocaine business. One of the most publicized cases was the military takeover of the Bolivian government in 1980. It was called the "cocaine coup" because so many figures, including the president and his minister of the interior, were involved in trafficking. Prisoners were set free and records of drug cases were destroyed by the government.

Antidrug patrols in Bogotá carry out random searches on motorists in an attempt to stop drug trafficking, but widespread corruption prevents any real success.

In Peru, one of the biggest traffickers, known as the "godfather," was close to police and government officials at the highest levels. Colombian congressmen, diplomats, and naval officers have been charged with smuggling cocaine, and so has the commander of Panama's armed forces, General Manuel Antonio Noriega. There have been scandals linking a prime minister of the Bahamas, officers of the Honduran army, and Venezuelan defense ministers to the cocaine trade.

Fear and violence

It is not just money that creates power, it is also fear. Many journalists in Colombia and Peru have been threatened for writing about the drug gangs. Some have been murdered, and some have had to go and live in other countries. In this way the traffickers make it too dangerous to broadcast and write honestly about drug corruption.

Cocaine violence has completely changed Medellín, which was once a busy but peaceful industrial city. Suddenly, dead bodies began to appear by the roadside, and gunshot victims filled the hospitals. The murder rate rose until it was one of the highest in the world. A feud between the rival Medellín and Cali trafficking gangs killed over 120 people in 1988. Instead of studying or working, young men tried to copy the gangsters by getting rich quickly in the cocaine business. Many became paid murderers.

The violence has also affected small towns and villages in the countryside. According to farmers' organizations, cocaine traffickers own more than two million acres of agricultural land in Colombia. The traffickers built up small armies of trained gunmen to get rid of peasant families and rebel groups because they wanted complete control of trafficking territory. Members of the Colombian military have been accused of helping the traffickers in some of these areas, and of taking part in massacres.

Drug gangs, murdering over 120 people in 1988, have made Medellín one of the most violent cities in the world.

Politicians, too, are often frightened into silence by seeing so many mayors, congressmen, and town council members murdered. The leading candidate for the 1990 Colombian presidential elections, Luis Carlos Galán, was shot dead on his campaign platform. After this, many politicians said it would be better to talk to the traffickers, rather than risk more deaths by trying to fight them.

Traffickers and the justice system

In 1984, Colombia's minister of justice, Rodrigo Lara Bonilla, was shot dead by a gunman on a motor bike. The minister had accused Pablo Escobar, who is believed to be the boss of the Medellín group, of drug trafficking and of killing two detectives who had caught him with 39 kilograms of cocaine. Pablo Escobar was later linked to the murder of the minister, and to

A bomb severely damaged the apartment of Pablo Escobar, believed to be the "godfather" of drug trafficking in Medellín.

the deaths of several other Colombians who tried to fight drug trafficking.

Enrique Parejo, the justice minister who took over from Rodrigo Lara, continued to wage war on traffickers. He signed papers ordering that Colombians wanted for trafficking should be sent to the U.S. to stand trial. This is called extradition, and the drug lords fear it more than anything else. They know that in the U.S. it is virtually impossible to buy their way out of prison. So they even shot, and nearly killed, Enrique Parejo after he had left the ministry of justice and gone to live in Budapest, as Colombian ambassador to Hungary.

Threatening letters were sent to the people who were making the decisions about extradition. When an agreement between Colombia and the U.S. was being discussed, one member of the supreme court in Bogotá received a letter saying he and his family would be killed if a law was passed: "War and bullets come next. We are not afraid of corpses and press scandals. . . If the extradition treaty is not stopped, you will be responsible; your life, the lives of your friends, of all the members of your family are at risk. You will pay. They will pay."

> ". . . your life, the lives of your friends, of all the members of your family are at risk."

The extradition treaty was found to be against Colombian law, and thrown out. There was talk of trying to re-establish extradition a year later. Colombia's attorney general announced that he thought an old treaty should be used. Within a week, he too had been murdered.

In August 1989, a judge, a police commander, and the presidential candidate Luis Carlos Galán were all shot dead by the cocaine gangs within three days. The president of Colombia declared war on the traffickers and announced a new extradition law. Several traffickers were sent to the U.S. for trial. The drug gangs answered the introduction of the extradition law by killing another judge in Medellín.

Judges have received funeral wreaths and small coffins in the mail as warnings. Those working on cases connected with cocaine trafficking are offered a bribe or a bullet. Not surprisingly, very few important traffickers go to trial or to prison. If they do, they are often freed by frightened judges.

7

BY LAND, SEA, AND AIR

Cocaine traffickers have tried almost every method of smuggling imaginable. Small dealers often pay travelers to carry a few hundred grams on an airline flight. Sometimes groups get together to organize shipments of a ton or more. Experts calculate that by the late 1980s, South America exported about 400 tons of cocaine a year to the rest of the world.

About 75 percent of this went to the North American continent. The authorities probably captured ten percent or so, and the remainder was distributed in Europe, Australia, and the Far East.

Most flights are illegal ones made at night.

More and more countries have been drawn into the cocaine network as drug traffickers look for new routes out of South America. The Bahamas and other Caribbean islands, with their many deserted reefs and quiet inlets, are favorite stopovers for Colombian gangs. Small planes carrying cocaine to Florida refuel on rough airstrips, or transfer their cargoes to yachts and high-speed motorboats. The islands, which are also used by the traffickers as a stepping-stone to Europe, are being corrupted by cocaine money in the same way as the cocaine-producing countries.

United States authorities calculate that nearly half the cocaine transported to the U.S. arrives in private aircraft. Most flights are illegal ones made at night, and the planes land for just a few minutes on small, isolated strips. "El Loco," a

COCAINE

Bolivian who flew these routes, is a legendary figure in many smuggling stories. He was a bush pilot who flew alone and carried out his own navigating and repairs. One story tells how he managed to dodge fighters on a trip to Mexico in his DC-6. His career ended when he took off while drunk and flew straight into a mountainside.

Brazil, with its enormously long, unpopulated jungle frontiers, has become another shipping center for the cocaine trade. Cocaine from the Andean nations is sent from Brazil through to Europe, often via West Africa and Portugal, or northward to the U.S. Between 1981 and 1987, the amount of cocaine captured rose ten times, to 1,000 kilograms. Even so, Brazilian police knew that they were only stopping a tiny percentage of the flow. In mid-1988, four tons of cocaine were found packed into hollowed-out cedar beams that had been shipped from the Amazon River to Florida.

How cocaine is smuggled

Cocaine is often hidden in legal exports. It has been found in banana boats and furniture from Colombia, in crates of shrimp, and honey and chocolate from Ecuador. Cartons of freshly cut flowers sent from Bogotá have so often been stuffed with cocaine that nearly all the shipments are now searched. Often the cocaine is not in the product itself, but neatly hidden in the packing materials. One group of dealers set up a tropical fish business and put slabs of cocaine into the polystyrene walls of the boxes that they used to send the fish to England. The dealers were caught and imprisoned.

> *Cocaine . . . has been found in banana boats and furniture . . . in crates of shrimp, and honey and chocolate.*

Airlines with regular flights from South America have paid multimillion-dollar fines when cocaine has been found behind panels in the bodywork of planes. Now careful searches with dogs trained to sniff out drugs have made this method of smuggling less popular.

For big shipments, the gangs pay customs officers, policemen, and transportation workers to look the other way. The smaller-scale smuggler rarely has this kind of protection.

Cocaine is smuggled out of South America by almost every possible means. Here, boxes of flowers are being searched for hidden drugs.

South American newspapers often publish pictures of miserable-looking travelers of all nationalities who have been caught at airports with a kilo or so of cocaine. Couriers known as mules are paid to carry the white powder stuffed into false-bottomed suitcases, high-heeled boots, teddy bears, toothpaste tubes, or children's books. Clothes are sometimes soaked in cocaine solution, and people often strap packages of the drug to their bodies.

Couriers may take roundabout routes to try and confuse officials who are watching the direct flights from Colombia and Peru. For example, to reach the U.K. from Peru, a courier may fly from Lima to Santiago de Chile and to Buenos Aires before arriving in London. Similarly a smuggler may reach the U.S. from Colombia by flying from Bogotá to Caracas, to Puerto

COCAINE

Twenty-four one-kilogram packets of cocaine were found concealed in this car in Bogotá. This amount would have been worth about $2\frac{1}{2}$ million when smuggled into the U.S.

Rico and then to New York. Customs officers know what kind of people are likely to be carrying drugs. A typical cocaine mule is often a young woman who seems slightly out of place in fashionable new clothes, her ticket has probably been paid for in cash at a travel agency, and she does not have a permanent job.

In the early 1980s, cocaine prices reached $40,000 a kilogram for large-scale shipments in the southern U.S. However, so much was being produced that prices began to fall. By 1988, the price per kilo for a large cargo had dropped by over 75 percent.

Traffickers have been looking for new areas to sell larger quantities of cocaine and earn bigger profits. Concentrating on Europe, they have begun to use Spain as a business and shipping center. With plenty of flights, regular trade connections, and a shared language, the country makes an obvious stepping-stone for South Americans. The Spanish authorities found over a ton of cocaine in 1987, compared with only 15 kilos in 1978. Although cocaine use has increased enormously in Spain, most of each shipment is sent on by land to France, Italy, Germany, the U.K.,and the Netherlands. There are 56 flights a week into Madrid from South America. It is likely that there is at least one mule on each flight. Yet the custom officials expect to catch only four smugglers a week.

The traffickers and the authorities are constantly competing. To stay ahead, the traffickers change their routes and cover their tracks. A batch of cocaine may be transferred and repackaged several times on its journey. The authorities use radar to scan for illegal flights, together with coast guard patrol boats and trained agents to search cargoes, luggage, and travelers. However, according to one naval commander, stopping drugs from entering the U.S. is like trying to stop a missile after it has been fired. In addition to controlling air and sea space, patrols have to cover Mexico's long border with the U.S., which is a favorite route for smugglers. Most customs officers think they are doing well if they can capture one out of every ten kilos of cocaine smuggled from South America.

> *Most customs officers think they are doing well if they can capture one out of every ten kilos of cocaine smuggled from South America.*

There are occasional triumphs for the authorities. In 1987, a ship carrying containers from Colombia docked at Southampton, England, to unload coffee and cotton. Among the containers taken off the ship was one going on to Rotterdam in the Netherlands. A customs officer noticed that the bolts on the back of the container looked as though someone had tried to meddle with them. The container was quickly moved into a shed and opened. The inside had been repainted and seemed new compared to the battered outside.

Stacks of boxes holding ceramic tiles reached three-quarters of the way up the container. When an investigator tapped the roof, it was found to be false and had had secret compartments added to it. There were 64 packages of cocaine — 208 kilos in all — hidden in the container. Different kinds of packaging showed that the cocaine had come from six different Colombian laboratories.

Within seven hours, the customs officers had switched the cocaine to bags of grain and the container was back on the dock. The ship went on to Rotterdam via France and Germany. When it reached its destination the container was watched for a month before anyone tried to move it. Then it was followed to a trailer park, where three people were caught trying to open up the roof. In all, eight arrests were made as a result of cooperation between the customs and police of four countries — the U.K., France, Germany, and the Netherlands.

The mule

For three days, the Colombian stopped eating. He bought two dozen pair of surgeon's rubber gloves and cut the fingers off them. He put five grams of cocaine into the fingertips, doubled the rubber over, and tied it. Then each ball was re-wrapped inside another rubber finger. The balls were rolled in butter to make them easier to swallow. It took the man six hours to swallow 840 grams of cocaine in this way. He was paid $2,000 to carry the drug in his stomach on a flight from Colombia to Spain and, after several trips, he had saved up enough money to start his own business. Yet he knew he was one of the lucky ones, because soon afterward, a young American on a flight from Lima to the U.S. died when a cocaine-packed rubber balloon leaked into his stomach. The same year, at least 20 other mules were poisoned in the same way.

These rubber-covered balls containing cocaine were recovered from inside a captured smuggler.

8

COCAINE AND CRACK

Once cocaine arrives in the U.S. and Europe it is handled by a chain of dealers. Each person in the chain is out to make as much money as possible. Often Colombians receive the shipments from trafficking gangs and begin to distribute the cocaine. These wholesalers send out lots of five, ten, or even 100 kilos to other cities and countries.

> *Close relatives are often victims of the drug traffickers' revenge.*

By making their own people responsible for the first stage of distribution, the gangs increase their profits, reduce the risks, and make their operations more efficient. A Colombian knows that if he should try to cheat the organization, he will not have an easy death. Close relatives are often victims of the drug traffickers' revenge.

The dealers

When cocaine reaches the local dealers, they usually add some white powder to it to make the drug go farther. This is known as "cutting" the cocaine and can be very dangerous if the dealer mixes in another drug. Sucrose, a form of sugar, is one of the most common cuts, but aspirin, talcum powder, or flour may be used.

With the drop in cocaine prices, dealers cut it less. In the early 1980s a street dealer sold cocaine that was only ten percent pure. Now most street sales contain about 50 percent of the drug. The user cannot tell what has been cut in, or how pure the drug is. Somebody who normally buys 20 percent pure cocaine could be overwhelmed by the effect of an unexpected, stronger dose. It could lead to a heart attack.

A big dealer makes more money and takes fewer risks by staying far away from the streets. Often the dealer will have a few regular clients who buy a kilogram or so of cocaine at a time. These clients have other clients, and gradually the cocaine is broken down into smaller packages until it reaches the street, where the neighborhood dealer, or pusher, handles twists of paper containing a gram or less.

Most street sales contain about 50 percent of the drug.

By this time, the gram of white powder in say, Boston, costs nearly 50 times more than it did when it left the laboratory. In Europe the difference in price is even greater, and couriers sometimes take trips to the U.S. to buy cocaine to sell in London.

Drug dealers are in the cocaine business to make money, but in an illegal, violent business things can easily go wrong. The profits may be large, but the losses are too. Even one batch of cocaine stolen or seized by the police can leave a dealer bankrupt and serving a long prison sentence.

Not all cocaine ends up on the street. Dealers' networks have been uncovered in financial companies, factories, colleges, and sports clubs. Often people dealing a few grams to colleagues make very little profit — just enough to pay for their own "habit." In 1988, eight members of a New York school board were suspended for selling and using cocaine, as well as stealing school equipment to finance their deals.

Crack

Crack is the smokable form of cocaine. It takes a simple chemical process to turn cocaine into crack. A small New York dealer can triple his money in a few hours by turning his supply of cocaine into a larger amount of crack.

"Crack is a real street drug. It seems cheap, because such a small quantity can be bought, and it gives a tremendous high that passes quickly. A few years ago, crack was nowhere — now look at it," says one police officer.

Corpses, killed by rival gangs, are frequently seen in both North and South American cities that have a lot of drug dealers.

"A few years ago, crack was nowhere — now look at it."

Crack dealing and violence go hand in hand. In some cities, those who live in drug-dealing neighborhoods are scared to go out. The homes of people who criticize dealers and organize antidrug campaigns are attacked and people are killed. Sometimes angry residents of an area hit back. In Detroit a group of local people burned down one crack house.

Crack dealing and violence go hand in hand.

Violent crack dealing gangs throughout the United States have been responsible for some brutal killings. In cities such as Washington, D.C., the police say that over half the murders committed are connected to drugs. Even teenage dealers are often armed and fight their battles on the street. Ten- to twelve-year-old children are used as lookouts or messengers for crack dealing houses. Once in the business it is very difficult for them to escape from it. They can earn much more money than their parents, to buy gold jewelry and expensive clothes, but they soon become addicted to crack themselves.

Although there have been fewer crack captures in Europe, it is probably only a matter of time before this changes. Cocaine and crack are still expensive in the U.K., but crack is already being sold frequently by drug dealers in London.

Crack neighborhoods

The Tactical Narcotics Team — TNT — was created in New York City after the murder of a policeman in 1988. Police officer Edward Byrne was shot and killed while he sat in his patrol car, guarding someone who was prepared to give evidence in court against crack dealers. The witness's house had already been fire-bombed twice.

TNT units moved into neighborhoods with serious drug problems. Investigators and undercover police officers buy drugs in crack houses or on the street to get evidence against the dealers so they can arrest them. They pass on information to other police departments so they can chase the big dealers.

Crack is the smokable form of cocaine. It has been a major contributor to increased violence in the drug world.

A large demonstration in Bogotá called for a crackdown on the drug barons who have such control over the country. In 1989, a massive campaign was launched against them.

On its first day of operation, a TNT unit in the Harlem section of the city arrested 25 suspected drug dealers. Nearly 600 vials of crack were seized. Recently, say the police, cocaine paste, as well as crack, is being sold openly by Colombian dealers in the New York borough of Queens.

After TNT units have been operating in an area for several weeks, community leaders notice a big difference. However, when the unit moves on to another neighborhood, the drug dealers return and crack houses reopen. Although special courts have been set up to cope with drug cases, there is not enough room in detention centers, or in antidrug programs, to keep people off the streets.

Fear often keeps people from speaking out against drugs, so the New York police started a crack hotline in 1986. Anyone can phone in information without giving their name. At the police communications center, there is always at least one person answering the crack line. The officer gets as much detail as possible and immediately punches the information into a computer. A patrol car can be on its way within minutes.

There are about 100 calls a day on the hotline. Some of them come from people needing advice or treatment, but most give the police information about the street corner dealers from the crack houses.

THE HUMAN COST

Since the beginning of this century, cocaine has been illegal in the U.S., but it is only recently that people have come to realize just how dangerous it can be. They have seen the results of cocaine misuse and overdoses, and many famous people have joined antidrug campaigns.

Cocaine and its effects

The white crystalline powder, cocaine hydrochloride, is usually sniffed. Users occasionally inject a solution of the powder, but this is less common. Mixed with heroin and injected, it is known as a speedball. Crack is smoked in pipes or rolled with tobacco in a cigarette. Crack is absorbed into the bloodstream in a few seconds, and the effect wears off after about 12 minutes, more quickly than sniffed cocaine.

> . . . *physical effects include a dry mouth, sweating, and a lack of appetite.*

Cocaine is a stimulant. It speeds up the brain and the rest of the body's central nervous system. It makes the heart beat faster and raises both blood pressure and the temperature of the body. Cocaine affects different people in different ways, but the high is often accompanied by rapid breathing and a racing heart. Other physical effects include a dry mouth, sweating, and a lack of appetite. When cocaine is being sniffed, the nose becomes numb.

As the high begins to fade, the user often feels irritable,

and depressed and desires more cocaine. Unlike heroin and alcohol, stopping cocaine use does not produce drastic physical symptoms of withdrawal. However, people who use cocaine regularly feel distressed if the drug is unavailable; they no longer feel normal unless they have cocaine.

There are other physical effects. Coke sniffers often have nosebleeds and the inside of the nose gets sore, cracked, and ulcerated. Smoking irritates and damages the lungs and can lead to chronic bronchitis and more serious lung conditions. Injecting cocaine is even more risky. The substances used to cut cocaine go straight into the bloodstream. This means that blood clots and abscesses can form, and sharing needles can pass on fatal infections such as AIDS.

A 1987 study of emergency cases in U.S. hospitals found that over 45,000 were linked to cocaine, and overdose problems rose by seven times between 1983 and 1987. An overdose, caused by taking too much cocaine, makes the heart pound and skip beats. The skin turns very pale or grayish, and the person may gasp for breath and be shaken by sudden jerks or convulsions.

> *The skin turns very pale or grayish, and the person may gasp for breath and be shaken by sudden jerks or convulsions.*

An overdose can kill even if it is treated promptly. Comedian John Belushi died as the result of injecting a speedball. Len Bias, a young basketball star who did not apparently use cocaine regularly, died from sniffing too much cocaine. Heavy use can cause such depression that it leads to suicide, sometimes by deliberately taking an overdose.

Many people try cocaine because it is part of their social scene — at work, among friends, in college, or on the street. A businessman who ended up spending over $18,000 in a few months on cocaine said he came into contact with the drug through friends at parties. Then he found that he was addicted and needed it all the time.

Cocaine users are usually very talkative while they are high. They feel confident and think they are being clever, quick, and decisive. In fact, tests have shown that people do not really do things any better than normal with cocaine, they just feel as though they do. To try and avoid the jarring ups and downs,

Before becoming addicted to *basuco,* or cocaine paste, this Bogotá bootblack was poor but clean and healthy.

cocaine users, like the South American paste smokers, often drink alcohol and take other drugs at the same time.

"Wherever you have coke use, you have abuse," says Dr. McAuliffe of the Harvard Cocaine Project. "Sniffing or smoking, there's equal risk of addiction. It wears people out very fast." Few cocaine addicts manage to drop the habit altogether. If possible, people go into hospitals or special residential centers for several weeks, so that they can stay away from cocaine supplies. However, this kind of treatment is very expensive, and there are not enough rehabilitation centers that provide free treatment.

A year later, having become heavily addicted to paste, he is emaciated, dirty, and looks years older.

For any rehabilitation treatment to work, the addict must admit to being dependent on cocaine and really want to kick the habit. If their family is prepared to help, there is a much better chance of recovery. Friends who are not cocaine users, new activities, and support groups such as Narcotics Anonymous play a vital part in rebuilding an addict's life and self-confidence. Many addicts only admit they have a problem when their lives are ruined. Some may have reached the stage when they steal or turn to prostitution to buy cocaine.

Cocaine users may lose their health, their jobs, their homes, and their friendships, but they are not the only ones hurt by their habit. Society as a whole is hurt. Babies are born addicted and suffer because of mothers who smoked crack. People are killed in traffic accidents by drivers high on cocaine. Others live in fear of drug dealers and neighborhoods deteriorate. Cocaine abuse also breaks up marriages and families.

Cocaine users may lose their health, their jobs, their homes, and their friendships.

Breaking the habit in the young

Persuading people not to use cocaine at all is the most obvious way of stopping cocaine abuse. "You can't start drug education too young," says a drug counselor in Rhode Island. Even in kindergarten, children are now taught to take care of themselves and to look for healthy and positive things in life. Most schools have some sort of drug program, which is usually part of the health curriculum.

Discussing why people use cocaine, what harm it can do, and who uses it, helps children to understand some of the problems. A group of Rhode Island teenagers who receive special counseling because they themselves have had problems or live in drug-infested neighborhoods, expressed strong opinions on cocaine.

"You can't start drug education too young."

"You learn about it from other kids, and on the streets — not from teachers in schools," said one boy. "Sometimes you have no choice. There are kids who say every day, try it, try it, and beat you up if you don't."

In a neighborhood close by, residents told the police where to find the dealers. The police cleaned up the area, confiscating lots of crack, money, and weapons. Yet in a few weeks it was just the same as before. "They wave the stuff in your face," said one boy. For people who live in almost drug-free areas, saying no is much easier than it is when there is crack on every street corner.

Posters have been used in many parts of the world to try to dissuade people from using drugs.

Students in the fifth grade at the Sabatini Elementary School in Madison, New Jersey, created original antidrug rap songs that they hoped would get the message across to others and help to prevent drug abuse. This song is by Andrew and Michael:

I know this kid, his name is Mac
He asked me to come out back.

Mac said, "I got some great cocaine."
I laughed and said, "Do I look insane?"

Mac said, "If you take this stuff, you'll get high.
And then you'll kiss your worries goodbye."

I said, "If I took those drugs, yes,
I'd really lose my funkiness."

So just say to drugs, "I don't need you.
I've got lots more that I have to do!"

FIGHTING COCAINE

For a long time, countries have blamed one another for the cocaine problem. South Americans said that they would not be making cocaine if people were not buying it in the U.S. and Europe, while people in the U.S. criticized South Americans for not tackling the cocaine problem. Now it is becoming obvious that cocaine is everyone's problem, and blaming producers or addicts is pointless. Cooperation among police forces, among education agencies, and among governments is the only way cocaine can be fought effectively.

> *Now it is becoming obvious that cocaine is everyone's problem.*

Some people feel that stamping out cocaine is such a hopeless task that the drug should be legalized. The trafficking gangs, violence, corruption, and dealers would disappear, they say, because cocaine would no longer be a profitable criminal business. The money saved on customs controls, air and sea patrolling, and specialized police forces could be spent on treating cocaine addicts.

> *"The idea of legalizing cocaine is total insanity."*

Most people disagree with this. "The idea of legalizing cocaine is total insanity," says Dr. McAuliffe of the Harvard Cocaine Project. "People just don't have any idea of how destructive it is. Many more would try it if it was legal. They would kill themselves."

"There are no easy answers. We've got to do what we can, whether it is education or antidrug enforcement," said one police officer. "The cocaine problem is a reflection of our other problems, here and in South America."

A worldwide operation

Today, cocaine is being attacked on every front, from the Andean growing areas to the schoolrooms of North America and Europe. Pulling up coca bushes and burning them is impossibly slow, so chemical sprays are being tried out on coca plantations. Some people argue that the chemicals are not safe because they affect the crops alongside coca and may cause ecological damage. They also argue that this damage would spread, because as coca growers cut down more of the forest, greater areas of land would have to be sprayed. However, the cocaine makers are also responsible for an enormous amount of pollution. More than 150 streams and rivers in Peru are poisoned by chemicals from the laboratories.

In antidrug operations during 1988 and 1989, the Colombian authorities seized over 50 tons of cocaine and destroyed more

Captured cocaine and marijuana are burned by the antidrug squad after a successful drug bust.

than 1,000 labs. The police and army raided houses and farms owned by traffickers and seized planes, weapons, radio communications systems, and lab supplies. They found escape tunnels and complicated warning systems at houses owned by Pablo Escobar and other traffickers, but most of the cocaine chiefs got away.

More than 150 streams and rivers in Peru are poisoned by chemicals from the laboratories.

Controlling the chemicals used for making cocaine is an effective way of cutting production. Colombian companies importing ether and acetone have to have special licenses to prove that chemicals are being used in legal industries. However, there are still too many ways of getting around these controls, and ether and acetone are smuggled to the Andean countries from the U.S., Brazil, and Europe. The fact that more labs have been found in the U.S. recently shows that chemical controls are having some success. The traffickers are having to send paste to be refined in countries where the chemicals are more easily obtained.

In one joint U.S.-Colombian operation, two cigarette packet-sized radio transmitters were welded into the false bottoms of ether drums by U.S. agents. The drums were tracked by satellite to the Colombian Amazon, then planes took aerial photographs that showed a lab complex. Police found $12\frac{1}{2}$ tons of partly refined cocaine when they raided it.

In Australia in the first three months of 1988, 12 kilograms were captured, more than in all of 1987.

The amount of cocaine captured by customs and other agencies in the U.S., the U.K., Spain, and other countries reaches a new record nearly every year. Even in Australia, there are strong signs that cocaine is becoming a cause for concern. In the first three months of 1988, 12 kilograms were captured, more than in all of 1987. However, officials every-where say that more is being caught because more is being shipped, and they are still only finding between five and 15 percent of the total.

In Cauca, Colombia, an area badly affected by cocaine addiction, villagers act out dramas about the tragedy that drugs cause.

Community antidrug drives have made people aware that they can do something for themselves. From the villages of the Bolivian Yungas region to the shantytowns of Lima and the small towns of the U.S., there are campaigns to keep cocaine dealers out and help users to drop the habit. Former addicts contribute too, by telling of their terrible experiences and describing how easy it can be to become addicted without realizing what is happening.

Countries are increasing the fines and jail terms for cocaine use and trafficking. Carlos Lehder, a major Colombian trafficker tried in the U.S. in 1988, was given two life sentences plus 150 years. A user can now be fined up to $10,000 in the U.S. Drug testing by companies to make sure that their employees are "clean," or drug-free, is becoming more common. Both governments and private organizations have realized they need to spend more money on drug prevention and rehabilitation, and on specially trained antidrug forces.

However, isolated efforts by a few people or by one or two countries cannot achieve lasting results. The U.N. does its best to coordinate antidrug policies and also gives funds to programs in developing countries. Apart from projects to replace coca with other crops and efforts to improve the standard of living in coca-growing areas, the U.N. helps with

COCAINE

education and treatment. The U.S. Drug Enforcement Administration works with local police, supplying equipment and special training. Britain has sent trained dogs that sniff out concealed drugs in Ecuadorean airports and ports.

Some of the most successful joint international investigations have sent drug lords to jail. New agreements will allow bank accounts to be examined, and money belonging to traffickers will be seized. Already a number of people who do not actually handle cocaine but are responsible for channeling the profits into other businesses have been jailed.

Passing information through the Interpol (international police) network is becoming quicker with the use of computers. Tip-offs are less important than the steady flow of intelligence that allows customs officers and police to build up a picture of how the cocaine business works, who is in it, and where to find the evidence that will convict them.

The most dramatic ways of fighting cocaine — the sudden helicopter raid or the much-publicized trial of a top trafficker — are not always the most effective. Only the combined antidrug efforts of different groups and different nations can make people decide that cocaine is unacceptable and be effective in the fight against the drug and its abuse.

Trained dogs are used to sniff out concealed drugs.

INFORMATION

United States
National Clearinghouse for Drug Abuse Information
Office of Substance Abuse and Prevention
5600 Fishers Lane
Rockville, Maryland 20857

World Service Board of Families Anonymous
Families Anonymous Inc.
P.O. Box 528
Van Nuys, California 91408

Department of Education
Office of the Secretary, Room 4181
400 Maryland Avenue, SW
Washington, DC 20202

Massachussetts Department of Public Health
150 Tremont Street
Boston, Massachusetts 02111

Cocaine Helpline
Tel: 1-800-COCAINE (toll free)
Mon. – Fri. 9 am – 3 am
Sat. – Sun. 12 pm – 3 am

Canada
Addiction Research Foundation
33 Russell Street
Toronto, Ontario M5S 2S1

Alberta Alcohol and Drug Abuse Commission
10909 Jasper Avenue, 7th Floor
Edmonton, Alberta, T5J 3M9

INDEX

Library of Congress Cataloging-in-Publication Data

Kendall, Sarita.
    Cocaine / written by Sarita Kendall.
        p.   cm. — (Drugs — the complete story)
    Includes index.
    Summary: Presents information on cocaine and the serious problems it is causing today.
        ISBN 0-8114-3200-9   —   ISBN 0-8114-3205-X (soft cover)
        1. Cocaine — Juvenile literature.   2. Cocaine habit — United States — Juvenile literature. [1. Cocaine.   2. Cocaine habit. 3. Drug abuse.]   I. Title.   II. Series.
    HV5809.5.K46   1992
    362.29'8 — dc20   91-2781515
                                                                       CIP AC

Consultants: Kenneth J. Schmidt, Passaic County, N.J., Probation Dept.; Marilyn Devroye, consultant for Psychiatric Institutes of America, Washington, DC.

Editors: Margaret Sinclair, Gina Kulch

Cover design by Joyce Spicer

Typeset by Tom Fenton Studio, Neptune, NJ
Printed and bound by Lake Book, Melrose Park, IL

Photographic Credits
Cover: © James Minor, *inset:* © George H. Harrison/Grant Heilman, Inc.; 7 Zefa; 9, 12, 13, 16, 18a, 29 Sarita Kendall; 44 David Hoffman; 3, 48 David Browne / Rex Features; all others Timothy Ross Picture Group.

Original text and illustrations
© Heinemann Educational Books Ltd. 1991